Create your own
LOVE SPELLS

NoR

Please renew or return items by the date shown on your receipt

www.hertsdirect.org/libraries

Renewals and enquiries: 0300 123 4049

Textphone for hearing or speech impaired   0300 123 4041

520 700 31 5

Create your own
LOVE SPELLS

*Charms of enchantment to
entice and keep a lover*

LAURA J WATTS

LORENZ BOOKS

This edition is published by Lorenz Books,
an imprint of Anness Publishing Ltd, 108 Great Russell Street,
London WC1B 3NA; info@anness.com

www.lorenzbooks.com; www.annesspublishing.com

If you like the images in this book and would like to investigate
using them for publishing, promotions or advertising, please visit
our website www.practicalpictures.com for more information.

© Anness Publishing Ltd 2014

A CIP catalogue record for this book is available from the
British Library.

Publisher: Joanna Lorenz
Executive Editor: Joanne Rippin
Designers: Tania Monckton, Ian Sandom and Adelle Mahoney
Photographer: Don Last
Illustrator: Lucinda Ganderton

PUBLISHER'S NOTE
Some of the projects in this book use candles. Take care at all
times to ensure that candles are firmly secured and that lighted
candles are never left unattended. An effective flame-resistant
spray can be applied to displays, though this will not make them
fireproof. Any use to which the recommendations, ideas and
techniques are put is at the reader's sole discretion and risk.

PICTURE CREDITS
The publishers thank the following agencies for permission to
use their images in this book.
The Bridgeman Art Library – pp 7, 10, 11, 13, 17, 22bl, 27, 60,
and 61.
Fine Art Photographic Library Ltd. – pp 8, 9, 12, 40.

CONTENTS

INTRODUCTION

To love someone is to give yourself whole-heartedly, without expectation, and to receive openly, without judgement or reservation. Only your true self can love in this way. When ego or cynicism does not weigh you down, when you are not living in the past or in an imagined future, then you are at peace with yourself, and can love.

Love represents the heart, not the mind, and it can often defy the boundaries of reason. Love can express raw emotions, uncut and untempered by logic or analysis. It does not exist just to please another or yourself, it simply is.

Love is universal and connects all things. You need only to open your heart to feel the wellspring of love around you. Love charms are gifts that honour both you and your connection with the universe. That connection may be romantic love,

sisterly love or the love for an animal or flower. Making a love charm, filling its creation with your hopes, not your fantasies, with your unconditional love, not your desires, reminds you of who you are and where you are going.

A love charm is firstly a gift to yourself. Everyone is special. As you make the charm, it, too, becomes special. It represents your current thoughts and feelings, and when you give your love charm away, you pass on that respect and uniqueness. Giving a love charm is a sign that you truly honour and love a person.

ABOVE: *Love charms can be made from the everyday objects around you, or you can gather together a collection with a charm in mind.*

OPPOSITE: Romeo and Juliet, *1884 by Sir Frank Dicksee (1853–1928). A beautiful painting of one of the most potent love stories ever told.*

> Love is patient and kind; love is not jealous or boastful; it is not arrogant or rude. Love does not insist on its own way; it is not irritable or resentful; it does not rejoice at wrong, but rejoices in the right. Love bears all things, believes all things, hopes all things, endures all things.
>
> 1 Corinthians, 13 (4–7)

The Art of Giving

To give without expectation is the essence of a love charm. When you give something expecting something in return, you do not love wholeheartedly, you love conditionally.

Giving a love charm as a kind of transaction – for gratitude, forgiveness or promises – is an act of egoism, not of the true self. You are dishonouring yourself, the person to whom you are giving the gift and your relationship.

The joy of giving is never to want anything in return. Making a love charm is an act of unconditional expression. You are creating something that may have the briefest of existences; it may be given and forgotten or it may be treasured for a lifetime. It does not matter which and does not change how valuable the charm is or the intent with which it was made.

The Way to Give

A truthful person should not judge how a person receives a gift. In giving, you speak the truth of your heart and show the recipient your deepest love and honour. You may feel he or she has not heard, may not care, or may not even understand. This is the voice of your ego judging that person's response. In judging another person you show that you no longer trust or believe in him or her.

The making and giving of a love charm must be done with the whole self, which is who you are when you are not dwelling on the past or the future. You must live in each heartbeat, accepting every moment with pleasure.

LEFT: *Flowers have long been a token of love and affection and are given not only to lovers, but friends and family.* Tristan and Isolde, *1904 by Andrew Watson Turnball.*

> **"Yesterday's the past and tomorrow's the future. Today is a gift, which is why they call it the present."**
> BILL KEANE

The Art of Receiving

WHEN SOMEONE HONOURS YOU WITH A GIFT, HE OR SHE REMINDS YOU THAT YOU ARE SPECIAL, THAT YOU ARE UNIQUE IN THIS WORLD. YOU SHOULD RETURN THAT HONOUR AND ACCEPT THE GIFT WITH AN OPEN HEART.

The ego may say that you are not worthy or that you are too proud, but your true self feels the love inherent in the gift and will shine through, if you let it. The gift may be a compliment, a present, a touch or a simple glance. These gifts are offered to your heart so you should let it speak openly in reply.

You should give without expectation or judgement and you should receive gifts in this way. If you are responding honestly, without wanting something in return, then you do not have anything to fear. If you do not judge the gift, whether it is bought or handmade, whether it is large or small, then you see only the intent behind it. All gifts are equal. The difference is in how you perceive them.

Accepting Gifts

A gift is a beautiful thing and should be received with beauty and grace. A love charm captures the beauty in your heart. If you accept a love charm with the deepest honour and respect, so you honour and respect the giver.

Receiving is an art that has been lost to many; people sometimes feel self-conscious when someone pays a compliment, or can be suspicious of an invitation. They often choose to see only the shadows of a person's motives. The cynical voice inside the head drowns out the innocence of the heart. A world full of shadows is a dark place. Let go of your fears and accept with wisdom and not question the intent behind a person's gift. Look for only the light of his or her heart's intentions.

You are given each day as something new to experience. All you have to do is accept it for the gift that it is. Gifts also come from people's hearts and fill your everyday life, whether they be a simple smile, friendly words, a touch or the offer of food or help. It is up to you to accept these things and see them for what they truly are, a love charm for your own unique heart.

LEFT: *Gifts do not have to be of material value: gestures and kindnesses are of great value.* The Kiss *by Sir Lawrence Alma-Tadema (1836–1912).*

Love Charms in Legends

Tales of love charms are woven into the myths and legends of every culture, and show how a spell, song, sacred object or creature strengthens the connection between two people to draw them closer together.

In Celtic mythology, the hero, Diarmuid, had a beauty spot on his cheek which enticed Gráinne, the wife of his chief to run away with him. He refused her love until she put a *geasa*, a word of power on him, and he became her lover. The *geasa* is a love charm, a simple word, which if spoken from the heart can give birth to something new and passionate. Words can have the power to bring love to life.

Sometimes your voice is not one of words but one of song. In a Native American Sioux myth, a young, lonely hunter became lost in a forest. As he tried to rest, he heard a beautiful, ghostly sound that made his heart ache, and he was led by a woodpecker to its source. He found a cedar branch full of holes hammered out by the bird, and heard the high, haunting song as the wind blew through it. Reverently, he brought this roughly-made flute back to his people and composed a special song for his *winchinchala*, his sweetheart. Its beautiful sound transfixed her, bringing her to him and she agreed to marry him. The Sioux regard the flute as an instrument for speaking to the heart of a loved one.

Love charms can also symbolize the eternal and spiritual nature of love. According to legend, Tristan, nephew of King Mark of Cornwall, and Iseult, his future Queen, mistakenly drank a love potion intended for the King. They fell deeply in love and for a time the lovers met in secret. The King discovered their affair and Tristan left for voluntary exile in Brittany. Eventually the tragic pair were buried side by side and, above their graves, two yew trees grew so close together that they became entwined. Yew trees regenerate and in many religions they are thought to aid the passing of a soul from death into a new life. Love, like the yew tree, is also part of an eternal cycle of birth, death and rebirth, and only by accepting that cycle will you be able to love forever.

In Greek mythology, the goddess of love, beauty and fertility, Aphrodite, often used spells and charms to do her mischievous work on the gods and mortals alike. She is an iconic figure, born from the foam of the sea and is often depicted rising from the waves. Her charms often had poor consequences, as she frequently seduced men and exerted her heavenly powers to satisfy her own erotic pleasure, and not her heart. She was said to charm the god of war, Ares, into her bed, but was caught by her husband, Hephaistos. Zeus, the ruler of the gods, punished her infidelity by forcing her to sleep with a mortal.

Cupid was the Roman god of love and the son of Venus, the Roman goddess of love. He was often depicted as a cherubic, but capricious and wanton boy, armed with a quiver full of "arrowed desires" or a torch to inflame love in the hearts of gods and men. Some of his arrows, however, would turn people away from those who fell in love with them.

According to one myth, Venus was jealous of the beautiful mortal, Psyche (Greek for "soul") and told Cupid to make her love the ugliest man alive. But Cupid fell in love with Psyche and hid her in a secret place where he could visit her every night. He told her never to try to see his face, but one night she lit a lamp and saw Cupid beside her. He reproached her and fled, fearing what his mother might do to him now that his secret was discovered. Psyche searched the world for Cupid, until the god Jupiter granted her immortality and gave her in marriage to Cupid.

Love charms have as much potential to do harm as to do good; what goes around, comes around. You should be willing to receive similar vibes to the ones you generate.

Fairytale Love Charms

In the tale of *Beauty and the Beast,* it was the charm or gift of a rose that brought the two lovers together. A man picked the rose for his daughter, Beauty, but the beast, who owned the rose bush, demanded her life in exchange for the gift. Beauty agreed to live with the beast in his castle and in time came to care for him. One day, she left to see her father, but the beast began to die without her. She rushed back to declare her love for him, and in so doing released him from a spell and he became a prince. The rose brought the two lovers together, but it was the words that Beauty spoke which transformed their love and brought it to life.

This act of declaring love, of giving wholeheartedly, is so magical and powerful that fairytales abound with it. The frog-prince was transformed by the kiss of a princess. In the story of *Sleeping Beauty*, she was woken by the kiss of a prince, as she lay surrounded by enchanted rose thorns. By expressing what is in their hearts, everybody has the capability to transform someone else.

The story of Cinderella has many roots. One of them, Grimm's *Aschenputtel*, is a story of how a love charm can motivate someone to fulfil a heart's dream. Aschenputtel planted a hazel twig on her mother's grave. A tree grew and a dove came to nest there. One day a prince invited her ugly stepsisters and her to three balls. On the first night, she was left behind and she sat under the tree in despair. The dove heard her crying and it fetched her a dress as a gift to wear to the ball. She went to each ball and danced with the prince.

After the third ball, in her rush to get home, she left a slipper behind. The prince visited every house looking for her. Finally he was united with Aschenputtel. The dove was the charm that spoke to her and acted to bring their love together. But it was only because she was looking for love that the dove's message was heard. A love charm may sound in the smallest moments; you should always try to listen for its call.

The fairytale of Rapunzel tells of how love can heal the deepest wounds. A witch locked Rapunzel in a high tower, but she was visited by a prince who climbed up her long hair to her window. One day, the witch found them together and threw the prince from the window. He fell on to a patch of thorns and was blinded. The witch sent Rapunzel to a land far away. Years later, the prince, who had been blindly wandering, heard her singing, and they were reunited. Rapunzel's tears of joy cascaded into the prince's eyes, healing his lost vision.

Our love has the potential to heal the person we love, if we let it overflow from our hearts.

TOP: *From* Beauty and the Beast *by Edmund Dulac (1882–1953).*

OPPOSITE: The Sleeping Beauty *by Thomas Ralph Spence (1855–1918).*

RIGHT: Rapunzel, *1908 by Frank Cadogan Cowper (1877–1958).*

SYMBOLS FOR LOVE CHARMS

THERE ARE MANY SYMBOLIC OBJECTS THAT CAN BE USED WHEN MAKING LOVE CHARMS, SUCH AS
DIFFERENT TYPES OF TREES, ANIMALS, FLOWERS OR STONES. SYMBOLS OF THE SOUL INCLUDE
LESS LITERAL THEMES, SUCH AS PATTERNS, WORDS OR MOTION.

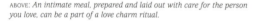

ABOVE: *An intimate meal, prepared and laid out with care for the person you love, can be a part of a love charm ritual.*

FOOD AND LOVE

Love charms and rites have always been used to find love and woo a true partner, whether deliberate or subconscious. Food is especially symbolic. Fruit, as a rich fertility symbol, has been used often in courting rituals. Many foods have a meaning, it might come from their shape, colour, taste or history. Apples have long been symbolic of love and fertility.

Giving food and the act of cooking for someone you love can be a charm or means of seduction. Baking a cake or cooking a delicious symbolic meal for a person you love, is as important today as it was hundreds of years ago. Wedding cakes have been a symbol of love for centuries and sharing the cake at the ceremony is significant of sharing love. The same symbolism can be part of the courting process too.

TEA

As part of the elaborate courting rituals of China the man would give the woman and her family *cha-li*, or tea presents. Tea, along with other gifts, such as sugar, wine, tobacco, cake and poultry, was presented and distributed by strict etiquette. Making tea for someone is an everyday event today, but even simple tasks can become a ritual and are important when imparting or sharing love.

APPLE PIPS

In medieval England an apple would be cut in half and the pips counted. An even number of pips would indicate that a new love would lead to a happy marriage. An odd number was a sign that the woman would remain unmarried for some time. If a pip had been cut through, then the love would be stormy and ultimately faithless, if two pips had been cut then the love was doomed to fade.

Trees

Trees and plants hold particular symbolic meanings and can be useful charms during courtship. Their leaves, the places they grow, the way their branches reach to the sky, can all have some relevance to your lives and love if you see it.
By walking through a forest and noticing how each tree is different, you can find something that speaks to your heart personally, and the branches, bark, leaves or fruit of a tree can be used in creating an individual love charm.

Beech

Beech bark was the first paper used for writing magical inscriptions. If you find some beech bark or wood, you could use it as part of an ancient wishing spell. Inscribe the wish on the bark, or carve it into a beech stick. Bury it into the ground to manifest itself as the wood decays and is reabsorbed back the Mother Earth. Just as the bark is consumed by the earth, so the wish will be released into the world and begin to show itself in your life.

You could also try carrying small pieces of beech bark in your pocket for luck and success in your love life.

Hazel

The hazel was believed to be the tree of knowledge and wisdom, and hazelnuts were revered as the food of gods. Hazel is a symbol of marriage, abundance of wealth, and family happiness. The hazelnut is said to be a symbol of peace and health and a source of wealth and power. In rural communities at Hallowe'en, a lover would take two hazelnuts, one for each person, and throw them into a fire. If they lay there quietly side by side, the match was deemed faithful, but if one nut moved away from the other, it was believed that one of the pair was unfaithful at heart.

Birch

Birch wood is believed to ward off evil, banish fears and build courage. Associated with beauty and tolerance, the Birch's vibration heightens tolerance of yourself and others. Birch is a tree symbolizing the birth of something new. In pagan times, silver birch was especially revered as a tree of feminine creation and wisdom. A Welsh ritual called for a man to weave a garland of birch wood and leaves and give it to the woman he loved. If she reciprocated his feelings, she would return the favour and present him with a garland. The garlands were a pledge of their love.

MISTLETOE

A parasite plant that grows on oak trees – themselves a symbol of fertility – mistletoe is a magical and sacred plant. Druids believed it had the power to cure illnesses, and ensure fertility. It was also believed to be an aphrodisiac, or sexual symbol, and the "soul" of the oak. It was gathered at midsummer and winter solstices, and the custom of using mistletoe to decorate houses at Christmas is a survival of Druid traditions. The ancient Greeks also thought that mistletoe had mystical powers, and in the Middle Ages if a couple in love exchanged a kiss under the mistletoe, it was interpreted as a promise to marry.

In Scandinavia mistletoe is considered the plant of peace, under which enemies can declare a truce.

Use mistletoe in a love charm to promote harmony, mend an argument, suggest passion and romance, or make a declaration of commitment.

APPLE

The apple tree is a symbol of love and peace. Offering an apple or apple blossom is a display of timeless love. In the Old Testament the Song of Solomon refers to the apple in a sexual context, and in classical Greece it was a symbol of beauty. If a young woman accepted the gift of an apple from a man she accepted his love. The Norse goddess, Iduna, and the Greek god, Apollo, both protected an apple tree laden with the golden fruit of immortality and youth. In Celtic mythology apples were associated with good luck.

Irish folklore says that if an apple is peeled in one continuous ribbon, and thrown over the shoulder, it will land in the shape of your true love's initial. Try this yourself and make a wish as you throw. Apple wood can be carved into amulets and talismans for love and longevity. Apple blossom can be scattered to mark a place as sacred to love.

HOLLY

The holly is a guardian tree. Its sharp, spiky leaves protect its red berries. Mistletoe is often found growing close to holly in mid-winter and the two plants together symbolize male and female fertility. Weaving a garland of holly and mistletoe is still a custom at Yuletide today. Holly is also seen as a healer of the heart, and in Bach remedies it is used to help those who feel unloved.

> "LOVE IS LIKE A TREE: IT GROWS BY ITSELF, ROOTS ITSELF DEEPLY IN OUR BEING AND CONTINUES TO FLOURISH OVER A HEART IN RUIN. THE INEXPLICABLE FACT IS THAT THE BLINDER IT IS, THE MORE TENACIOUS IT IS. IT IS NEVER STRONGER THAN WHEN IT IS COMPLETELY UNREASONABLE."
> VICTOR HUGO

FLOWERS

These are beautiful and transitory. They are a symbol of opening, awakening and passion. Through its colour, a flower calls out to be pollinated, to join with its fertile partner. We give flowers to call out to one another, to speak our hearts to people. Oils from flowers, such as camomile, jasmine and lavender, can be used for wonderful aromatic love charms, while giving a single stem flower, such as a rose or lily can be a simple love token all by itself.

ABOVE: *Roses and other flowers have great symbolism in romance, and have been the gifts of lovers for thousands of years.*

ROSE

This is a timeless symbol of love and regeneration. The first red rose was supposed to come from the blood of Aphrodite, the Greek goddess of love, who trod on a white rose and bled. Death symbolized by a white rose can lead to new life and love (the red rose). The thorns of the rose and its blood-red colour are reminders of the pain of being reborn. Letting go of the past is a difficult but necessary part of opening the heart to the possibility of new love to come. The rose is also a token of accepting love unconditionally.

LILY

The lily gives off a pungent perfume that can stimulate the heart. The white flowers are symbolic of purity, peace and innocence. It was said that lilies grew up where drops of milk from the earth goddess, Hera, fell to the ground when she created the Milky Way. The lily was sacred to the ancient eastern goddess, Astarte, symbolizing the rebirth of love and life at that time of year. The lily can bring a return to innocence and peace after a storm. It is a reminder that mistakes offer a chance to learn and be renewed.

LOVE RITUAL

THE NEXT TIME YOU ARE IN THE COUNTRYSIDE, A PARK OR EVEN A FLOWER SHOP, TAKE THE TIME TO SMELL THE SCENT OF THE FLOWERS AROUND YOU. NOTICE WHAT EACH SCENT BRINGS TO MIND: A MEMORY OR A SENSATION. FIND A PERFUME THAT REMINDS YOU OF SOMETHING JOYFUL, AND PLACE A BUNCH OF THOSE FLOWERS SOMEWHERE SPECIAL IN YOUR HOME OR GIVE THEM TO THE PERSON YOU LOVE.

ANIMALS

The animal kingdom was considered to be wise and a source of guidance and understanding. An animal can touch our spirits. Particular animals may already have meaning for you, for example, a bird that is nesting nearby or the memory of a dolphin at sea. What you feel and associate with those moments can help you find what you are looking for.

HORSE

Revered by the North American Indians the horse is seen by shamanic traditions as symbolizing love and devotion, loyalty and freedom. To the early Assyrian and Mongolian cultures the horse was central to survival in almost every aspect of their nomadic lives, and so represented a level of dual dependency and mutual love, similar to a marriage. In north European traditions the horse is also seen as a symbol of fertility.

DOVE

The dove is a monogamous bird, which may be the source of its connection with romantic and eternal love. The dove is also associated with peace and rebirth, and its feathers can be used in love charms. In ancient Greece the dove was sacred to Aphrodite, the goddess of love, and of Venus, her Roman counterpart, and it was a dove that told Noah that new life could begin after the Great Flood, bringing God's love back to man.

SEAL

Tales of these creatures, so agile in the water but clumsy on land, abound in Celtic mythology, such as the Selkie who came ashore on certain nights and shed their skins to become beautiful women until they returned to the ocean at dawn. Seals are symbols of change, of the wisdom that comes from within, and reminds us that to live with love and beauty you must accept and celebrate that the person you love will constantly change.

SWAN

Like the dove the swan is a bird that mates for life. The white swan is seen as divine, closely associated with purity, love and amorousness. The swan is also a symbol of transformation, both Zeus and Brahma were turned into swans to give birth to the world, and the fierce Norse Valkyries wore magical swan-feather cloaks during their rides from Valhalla. By accepting the transformation of love you can accept and respond to its passion.

Stones

Rocks and stones are formed under great stress and earthly forces. Each stone on a beach is different; some appear to have faces or animals staring out from them. Giving a stone as a love charm is an ancient ritual. A stone from your garden can be as special as one set in an engagement ring.

Diamond

Literally translated from Latin, diamond means world goddess. It is the hardest mineral substance known on Earth and is said to rule all other stones. In Tibet, the world goddess was reincarnated as a diamond, and this association with a virgin goddess developed into its symbolism as a new beginning. It is a symbol of indestructible love, a modern assocation that developed when it was declared as a token of romantic love.

Pearl

The shimmering pearl, and its spherical shape, is associated with the cycle of the moon and with the circle of eternity. It was believed that a pearl was formed when lightning struck the eye of a shellfish. Lightning is a powerful symbol of wisdom, and pearls are a sign of understanding. In ancient Greece, pearls symbolized love and marriage; wearing them promoted marital bliss and prevented newly wed women from weeping.

Ruby

The ruby's rich, deep-red rose, carmine or even purple colour symbolizes vitality and passionate love. Its richness was thought to overcome sickness and disease by cleansing the wearer of negative emotions and feelings. The ruby raises feelings and thoughts from fear and sadness to love and joy. It arouses the senses, stirs the imagination, and is said to guarantee health, wisdom, wealth and success in love.

Crystals

Much more affordable than precious stones, crystals are thought to have power and influence over our lives in many ways. Several crystals are associated with love, especially rose quartz, which is said to attract new love or renew existing relationships. Try placing a rose quartz under your pillow to stimulate love in your life. Green aventurine is said to attract love, while rhodocrosite teaches you that you are worthy of love.

Words and Letters

The act of writing or carving symbols and words was considered sacred and extremely powerful by many old cultures. When you hold a word or symbol in your mind and commit that permanently into the world by transcribing it, you are transferring your thoughts into reality. Inscribing a special mark, word or phrase into an object can help you to communicate your dreams to the world and, by destroying that object, allow you to let go of past dreams.

Love Ritual

Think of a phrase, a line in a poem or a saying that has some personal meaning for you. Take the first letter of each word and spend some time arranging them on a page. Create a pattern with the letters, perhaps linking them in a circle. You can use use runes if you wish for this ritual.

ABOVE: *Using runes for the love ritual above will give an additional level of symbolism.*

Runes

The Norse runic alphabet has many letters which can be combined together to create a single symbol. Each letter had some deep significance, which was used for divination as much as writing. For example, *Ansuz*, or mouth, is the letter for speaking and communicating. *Gyfu* is the letter for giving: its shape of a cross symbolizes the connection between two people. *Beorc* is the rune for new beginnings. Other runes that may be useful in creating a love charm are given in the table of runes on page 62.

Inscription

Inscribing words or a phrase, or even just a date, on to an object is a wonderful way to endow that object with memories and dreams. Engraving has always been common for jewellery, when given as a present or token, to be inscribed with secret words or a poem that would be understood only by the wearer. Any gift can be made unique by writing, carving, painting, or stitching on it some words of special meaning. The words can transform any object into a symbol of love.

Monogram

Taking the initials of two people's names and drawing those letters entwined together symbolizes their union. Spend some time designing a monogram for your relationship. Let your feelings express themselves freely in the contours of the letters. Consider all the unique ways in which your two lives overlap and shape those into the monogram.

Creating something that uniquely defines your relationship is a symbol of your active intent to entwine your two lives together.

Patterns and Pictures

The image and its associated meaning contained within a picture or pattern can sometimes communicate something deep inside you. A landscape from a holiday, a sunset on a beach, or the wings of a butterfly can all have deep significance. Pictures have been used to express feelings throughout history. Giving a picture as a symbol of the journey you are sharing with someone is a profound way of honouring your path together.

Shapes

The outline of a shape, the number of its sides and its colour can have special significance if you choose. The perfect symmetry of a circle is a timeless symbol of eternity. The crescent moon and its thirteen phases is a symbol of balance: light against dark, reminding us that all things wax and wane naturally. The sides and points of a triangle represent the three aspects to life and youth, maturity and learned wisdom. The five-pointed star speaks of brightness and passion. The square is a symbol of equality and strength.

Knots

The Celts used a sacred love knot to tie two people together. It was said to cast a spell over the lovers until the knot was untied. The intricate designs of the Celtic knot are never-ending lines, symbolizing the eternal nature of life and love. The Celts often used animals in imagery, their mouths holding their tails, creating a design of writhing creatures. Weaving a pattern using two threads is a sign of sharing your path with someone. Folktales from all over the world tell of women seeking to bind her lover by tying knots in a ribbon or girdle.

Spirals and Circles

The first shape used in art was the spiral, and it appears in every ancient culture throughout the world. It is also the oldest symbol to be used in spiritual practices. It reflects the universal pattern of growth. The spiral helps us to accept the turnings and redirection of life, and in love can help us accept change.

Circles also hold ancient symbolism, and commonly represent unity, wholeness and infinity. A circle is often seen as a protective charm, and in the form of a ring is used as a love token.

ABOVE: *Hearts, and circles – indicating rings – are closely associated with love and marriage.*

21

MOVEMENT AND TOUCH

The way you move your body speaks more intuitively and honestly of your actions, thoughts and feelings than any symbol. Your touch, the way you smile and the rhythm of your dance are the truest symbols of your feelings. Your body is a doorway through which you express your soul, your fears, your hopes and your love.

LOVE RITUAL

WHEN YOU ARE WITH SOMEONE YOU CARE ABOUT, ASK HIM OR HER IF THEY WOULD LIKE A HUG. IF HE OR SHE ACCEPTS, HUG HIM OR HER WITH YOUR HEART BEATING AGAINST ONE ANOTHERS. IN THOSE MOMENTS, THINK ABOUT HOW YOU FEEL ABOUT THAT PERSON AND TRY TO LET YOUR BODY EXPRESS THOSE THOUGHTS. A HUG IS A WONDERFUL GIFT OF JOY, COMPASSION AND LOVE.

ABOVE: *Music and rhythm have helped people express their feelings since the earliest times, as on this 5th-century Greek vase.*

DANCE

When you move your body in time and in step with the person you love, you are communicating on the deepest level. Many cultures see dance as the doorway to wisdom and knowledge. If you let go and give yourself to the dance, if you forget about performing in front of other people or behaving for someone else and let every muscle respond, you are letting your body naturally call out to your soulmate. Your soulmate is the person who can understand your dance and the expression of your body, and respond to you intuitively. Give in to the moment, and if you feel like dancing, dance, no matter where you are.

TOUCH

The magical gift of touch, the sensation of another body pressing its warmth against your own, is profound. The touch of a person's hand can open something deep inside you. Often, the touch of another can help you to release something. Touching someone can be both healing and sensual, such as when giving a massage. Touch offers comfort and reminds you that you are not alone – it can make you feel wanted, needed and that you are part of the world – whether a tribe, a culture, or a family – and always a part of the Earth. Touch can hold all kinds of subliminal messages and signals, as long as you are open to them.

Seasons and Cycles

Different times of the year had huge symbolism in the past. Each season was linked to life shared with the land. Even today, our bodies respond to light and temperature, so that we tend to be reflective by the fire in winter and active in the sun in summer. Choosing a time to give a love charm within these cycles can give it another level of significance.

Wheel of the Year

The Celts believed that all things begin in darkness, in winter, which is a time for letting go of the old and welcoming in the new. It is a time of accepting the past, a time of forgiveness and a time for wounds to be healed. In winter, you dream of the year to come. Spring is the season of awakening and preparation and when you express the dreams of winter. May Day, at the end of spring, was the traditional day to be married. In summer and the time of passion, you reap what you have sown. Then, during the embers of autumn you reach a peace with all those around you, and begin the cycle again as winter approaches once more.

Thirteen Moons

A woman's menstrual cycle is closely connected with the waxing and waning of the moon. It takes 13 nights for the moon to grow from new to full, which gave the number 13 its auspicious reputation, and the full 26 days is the length of a menstrual cycle. At the full moon, a woman is often ovulating and at her most fertile; this is a time of new beginnings when her body might become filled with life. The new moon, the dark moon, was considered by the Celts a time of death and rebirth; it was often when a woman would withdraw to begin menstruating during her "moon time". This is a time of initiation, wisdom and learning.

ABOVE: *Winter is a time to review the year and regenerate your own inner energy, just as nature renews and hibernates.*

Love Ritual

During the morning, write down your wishes for the day ahead. Put it to one side. In the evening, read the list and remember those that you made come true and those that never happened. Forget about all of them, let them go, and focus on the moment you have there and then.

Marriage Charms

There are many different marriage charms and gifts exchanged between men and women across the world to symbolize commitment. The tradition of giving tokens of love to one another in a marriage ritual has existed for centuries and the objects exchanged are deeply significant.

Rings

The giving of a ring to symbolize a marriage bond derives from the Anglo-Saxon ceremony where a woman transferred her lands to a house-man, or husband. The man would hand the woman a ring along with his wealth and declare that he would worship and honour her. The wife would then accept the ring, as a token of their eternal union, and agree to the familiar vows, including the now unused phrase, "to be bonny and buxom in bed". The marriage ceremonies of many cultures include the giving or exchange of rings and other items of jewellery, but the type of wedding ring and finger on which it is worn varies.

Lock of Hair

Hair is a deeply personal and expressive part of your body. Ownership of a person's hair was considered to impart a magic bond between two people. In Ireland, a man would offer a woman he loved a woven bracelet of hair, which, if she accepted, symbolized their permanent connection. In more recent times a lock of a lover's hair, curled into a circle, would be kept in a love locket. The circle of hair, like the woven hair bracelet, indicated a love that was eternal and timeless. This attitude sentimentally manifested itself in the custom of a widow's mourning jewellery, which was made out of the hair of her dead husband.

Pine Trees

In Scandinavian countries the pine tree has been a symbol of fertility for centuries. In Denmark an arch of pine branches, known as the Gates of Honour, is still sometimes constructed in front of the bride's home. In Norway friends and neighbours of the couple plant two small pine trees either side of their front door as a symbol of fertility.

Veils

The veil at a wedding originally symbolized the bride's virginity, innocence and modesty. Roman brides wore a flame-coloured and fulsome veil, called the *flammeum*, intended to protect the bride from evil spirits. In some Middle Eastern and Asian cultures a veil is worn to hide the bride's face completely, only to be lifted after the wedding is complete.

JUMPING THE BROOMSTICK

The custom of jumping the broomstick goes back many hundreds of years. A man and woman would take each other's hands in front of a witness, their grasp forming the symbol of eternity. They then jumped over a broomstick of birch twigs to symbolize letting go of the past and bringing in the new.

This common-law marriage was widespread in Britain until the 16th century. Broom jumping can still be found in Afro-American weddings, a reminder of when a marriage between slaves had no legal status.

FLOWERS AND GARLANDS

Wedding bouquets, wreaths and garlands are a feature of weddings in many different cultures as a symbol of happiness. Originally, bridal wreaths and bouquets were made of herbs with magical definitions for the couple's future life together. Celtic bouquets included ivy, a symbol of fidelity, thistle and heather, sage brought wisdom, dill lustiness. Later, bridesmaids carried sheaves of wheat, a symbol of fertility and renewal, and then flowers were introduced, orange blossom for happiness and fertility and lilies for purity.

DECORATED SQUASH

Taking the time to create a gift for someone is a powerful action. In the Slavic region, a man wanting to propose properly to a woman would present her with an earthenware pot containing pumpkin. The pot was a sign of permanence and would be displayed over her hearth, should she welcome his courtship. The squash were symbols of love and fertility, and was decorated with stones. If the woman consented to be his wife, the stones became a anklet, symbol of her status as a married woman.

WHEAT AND RICE

Wedding cakes, made from wheat, are another symbol of fertility, and were originally simple buns that were thrown rather than eaten to bring good fortune to the couple. It was the Romans who changed the buns into edible little cakes that were consumed as part of the ceremony. Showering the couple with grains of wheat, or in other cultures, rice, continued the tradition, while cakes became larger and much more elaborate. In the mid-17th century it was considered bad luck if any guest did not eat a piece.

THE CYCLE OF LOVE

The art of giving a love charm is that of listening, both to yourself and to the person you are giving to. You must always be aware of the intent with which you are filling the charm, so that you are always giving from the deepest part of your heart and not from the demands of your ego.

The word charm stems from the Latin word for spell or song, *carmen*. The Roman goddess, Carmenta was known for her words of power and was credited with adapting the Greek alphabet for use with Latin. A charm was a song or incantation sung by a woman to exert her power, the power of words and love, over a man. Love songs and ballads remain extremely popular and are still sung to give messages of love to someone special. To charm your lover was to spellbind him and cause him to feel lovesick and to act more passionately. Love charms were associated with enchantment and the weaving of love between two people. Love charms are also an opportunity for you to express the changes and challenges that you face in love. It is a chance for you to look within yourself for an answer to the problems that may lie before you and present them to the person you love. In a busy and bustling world, love charms are a reminder of feelings that you need to share.

Love has always been considered an act of nature, a source of irrational behaviour, as when people feel irrevocably drawn together or suffer love sickness. Just think of some of the common expressions of irrationality that people use: to be mad about someone, blind-

ly in love, love to distraction, worships the ground he or she walks on. These feelings are all part of a cycle of love. Love can open you up to new possibilities and new dreams. You are always changed by its touch on your life. The Cycle of Love can be visualized as a wheel with four sections, as the year has four seasons. Winter is the season of dreams, Spring is the season of hope, Summer is the season of passion, and Autumn is the season of fulfilment.

The Season of Dreams is the start, the time when you are alone or feeling disconnected from your life. This is the time you focus on the dreams of love to come and what needs to change to bring that about. Then, as love begins to flourish , you enter the Season of Hope, the hope that your dreams are being fulfilled. This is the time of innocence and gentleness, moving slowly as your love deepens.

The next part of the cycle is the Season of Passion. Now you have opened yourself out completely to the other person you will feel safe enough to express your love from every pore of your body. When your passion peaks and balances, and you find that new possibilities have opened up and that you have been changed by your love, you will be moving into the Season of Fulfilment. Now is the time that love heals and renews you until you find you must let go of your old dreams and begin to dream again. And so the cycle keeps moving.

ABOVE: *The seasons of the natural world follow a cycle that can also be useful in expressing the development of love and emotion.*

SEASON OF DREAMS

LIKE WINTER, THE SEASON OF DREAMS IS A TIME OF HIBERNATION AND INTROSPECTION, WHEN YOU PAUSE FOR A MOMENT AND CONSIDER WHERE YOU WANT TO BE GOING AND WHERE YOU HAVE BEEN. WHAT WERE YOUR DREAMS? WHAT ARE YOUR DREAMS NOW?

The Season of Dreams can be a time when you are enjoying being alone, or a time when you realize that love has changed you. It is time to reassess your relationships and yourself.

In the Season of Dreams it is dark and you may feel frightened, angry, or impatient for something brighter and better to come along. However, in the darkness, you have an opportunity to imagine something completely new and different, to branch out in a new direction. Dreams are your guide – you can map them, or follow them, and they will lead you to the inner voice of your heart.

This is often a season of frustration, when you find that life is a little harder on you. You must find space in your life for yourself, get to know what makes you happy, what makes you sad, the daydreams you have, and the nightmares. All these dreams are voices from your heart telling you what you want next and what must heal before you can take the steps towards your goal.

The Season of Dreams is a time for taking stock of the lessons learned, using them to guide you in what you need next in life, whether it is a new love or the rekindling and transformation of an old love.

As with winter, it is a period of stillness and of waiting and of listening. This is a good time to be alone, even for just a short while, to notice how you feel in your life and your heart. Love charms will help you, as a path for finding your true inner self, which may have become muffled in the day-to-day of your life, or drowned in recent pain. These quiet, contemplative love charms are tokens of the dreams that you are forming for the future and for what has happened in the past that you must now relinquish.

LEFT: *Look inwards and examine your relationships in the light of the four seasons and the cycle of the year.*

RIGHT: *Relationships can be in constant state of flux, just like elements in the natural world. By communicating your feelings and remaining close, you can adapt to changes.*

DREAMS TAKE YOU ON A JOURNEY THROUGH YOUR CONSCIOUSNESS AND DESIRES, AND HELP YOU DISCOVER WHAT YOU NEED IN YOUR LIFE TO FIND LOVE AND HAPPINESS. YOUR DREAMS ARE THE CALLING OF YOUR HEART.

A Time for Focus

During winter, the Season of Dreams, you need to make some time to focus on your own needs, wishes and dreams. Take this time of rest and hibernation to look inwards and examine what it is that makes you happy, what your dreams and desires are and how central they are in your life. It is important thing to remember that you cannot help to make another person happy without being happy yourself.

Keep a notepad by your bed and write down any dreams you remember. Think about what they mean to you and what feelings they evoke. If they are dreams of seeking out something, think about what you were looking for. If it was a nightmare, were you being chased, and if so, by what and why did it make you afraid?

Note your daydreams too, events from the past which you miss, or possibilities for the future which you yearn for. Find some time alone and sit and imagine that the world is about to end in a few days. Think about it seriously (no one knows what will happen in the future). What would you want to see, to create, to be or do before that happened? What is it that you have always dreamed of but never been able to do? What are the unspoken dreams you carry with you? If they are

simple, or even if they seem impossible, write them down. Now gather up all those dreams and feelings and meditate on them. Which are the most important to you? Which ones make your heart beat faster? Which ones would make you feel happy? Which ones would you want to share with someone you love? Which ones would you want to do alone?

All these dreams could be possibilities that you can make happen. Each one could become true if you want it to; it is only a matter of accepting the consequences each might bring and learning from the mistakes along the way. Everyone possesses the power to make changes in their lives and, by imagining their dreams, they take that small step towards being truly happy within themselves.

These are your dreams for the coming cycle.

BELOW: *In winter there is time to reflect on your inner world, the night and day dreams we have can be sources of inspiration.*

BELOW: *Keep a notebook by your bed during the Season of Dreams, so that if you wake up you can quickly note down any details.*

BELOW: *In the morning, share your dreams with your loved one and discuss any feelings or desires that might surface.*

MEDITATION ON YOUR INNER VOICE

This meditation is for clearing the mind of day-to-day worries, allowing you to focus on your inner voice. Once you can quieten your mind, you can easily recognize the dreams and needs of your heart and express them in a charm. This may take some practice and your may be surprised at how loud and busy your mind is. Once you master this, do it with your eyes open, so that you can clear your mind no matter what the distraction.

 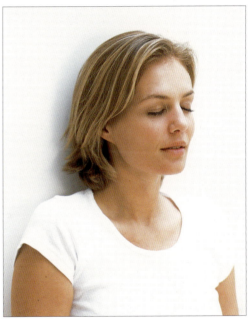

1 Before you begin, sit comfortably and relax. Think about your 'third eye'. Hindus believe this is located in the centre of our forehead, and that it is a gateway to inner realms. Now sit with your back straight, head up and your hands clasped and relaxed in front of you. Start with your eyes open. Notice the thoughts in your mind, the background noise, the sounds and smells around you. Breathe in slowly and count your first breath. Then close your eyes.

2 Now, as each thought comes into your mind, let it go again, do not dwell on anything. Let your thoughts become tranquil and your mind empty. Do not let your mind wander, focus on your body and on the moment. Breathe out slowly. Count ten slow breaths like this, just being and breathing in the moment with no thought of the past or future. Let yourself focus totally on the present; allow the clutter of your mind to fade into silence.

Dream Catcher Love Charm

A dream catcher is a Native American charm for capturing good, wise dreams
and for letting bad dreams pass through and away into the night. This is
a love charm for awakening the dreams both you and the person you
love hold inside your hearts.

Traditionally, a dream catcher is hung above a sleeping person's head, to keep wise dreams so that they can be remembered on waking and so that bad dreams can be forgotten. When you give your love charm, offer to help him or her hang it up and explain your intentions behind the gift. You could also spend some time listening to his or her dreams and sharing your own with your love. If this is a time of calling love into your life, hang the dream catcher above your own bed and devote some time to listening to your dreams.

When you make the dream catcher, spend a moment considering the wood or tree you want to use. Also think about what colour ribbon and wool (yarn) you feel would be most appropriate in the charm. Gather feathers that come across your path on a walk home for example.

The dream catcher has a single thread that is wound in a spiral from the outside to the centre, symbolizing the journey from the waking world to the world of dreams. The Native Americans believe that their dreaming selves pass through the heart of a dream catcher and return with knowledge of the dreams of their true selves.

LEFT: *The dream catcher is a charm to call in all the deepest dreams and desires of one's heart. It is a gift symbolizing the awakening of a person's heart and a willingness to follow his or her dream.*

You will need

Fallen branch
Sharp knife
Ball of coloured wool (yarn)
Coloured ribbon
2 or 3 feathers

1 Find a long, flexible branch from the place you choose and bend it into a circle. You may find you need to trim nodules and smooth the bark.

2 Slice across the branch at both ends so that they lie flat against each other. Secure the ends together using coloured wool (yarn).

3 Cover the circle with ribbon and fasten it securely at one end. This forms the simple outer loop of the dream catcher.

4 Tie the wool to the circle and wind it around the circle a few centimetres (inches) away, not too tautly. Repeat at equal distances around the circle. This is the spiral of thread that weaves into the centre.

5 When you have almost completed the circle, wind the wool around the centre of the next wool span. Repeat this spiral structure until you have a small central circle and then tie off the wool end.

6 Use the wool to secure feathers to your charm. They can be tied either to the branch so that they hang down from the dream catcher, or secured to a wool span, perhaps at the centre. Think about the person this is intended for and follow your instincts.

Dream Space Love Charm

This is a charm that creates a special place for love to rest. It is a place that reminds someone of all the wonderful dreams that love has and will fulfil.

At this time, in the Season of Dreams, you need to remember what has happened in your life, good and bad, and create new dreams to share with someone. A dream space is a shrine to the past and a dedication to the future. It is a physical space that you give over to your dreams, as a step towards your dreams physically manifesting themselves in your life. Think carefully about the place where you want to create the dream space. It should be somewhere you share with the person you love. Present the dream space love charm and all its intentions to the person you love. Light a candle with him or her in front of the pattern. Spend some time thinking and talking about those dreams. Think about what steps you might have to take to make them come true. Whenever you feel the need, come back to the dream space,

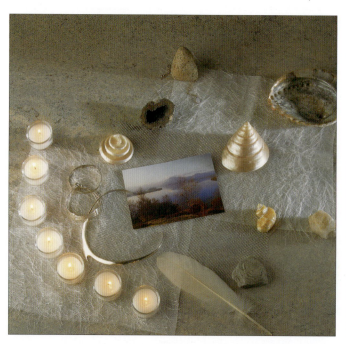

Crystals for Dreaming

Add to the power of your love charm with crystals, if you wish. Amethyst can be used for dream recall, and promote peaceful sleep and serenity. Clear quartz helps to amplify dreams, and help recollection. Aventurine can attract love and increase empathy. Rose quartz will help you accept and love yourself and will heal the heart.

You Will Need

Picture of a special place
Stones
A special item from a relationship (such as jewellery)
Candles

1 Find a picture that signifies something both of you dream of, something you want to share together in the future, a place you want to travel to perhaps. Think of dreams you have already shared together, and any special items you already have from those dreams. Gather some stones from a special place and focus on the future you want to create.

2 Place the stones around the picture in a shape or pattern that you feel represents your dreams. This may be a circle representing the eternal bond you share, or perhaps a star for the passion that you feel needs to enter into your life. Choose whatever shape feels right for you. Experiment with the pattern until it feels right. Add your other special items.

3 If you have a special item that links with the picture, you could place it above or below the picture, if you wish. Spend time focusing on where you want the picture.

4 Place the candles around the space, arranging them in a way you feel is appropriate. Remember never to leave burning candles unattended.

SEASON OF HOPE

In the Season of Hope new love is beginning to blossom. In the Season of Dreams you demonstrated your intention for change in your life and now something has been kindled, or resurrected, or it has simply altered its course towards your dream. It is a gentle time, where you must be patient and let the love grow slowly and delicately. It is not a time to rush into things but to realize the beauty and wonder of the love that has entered into your life.

During the Season of Hope you may be treasure-hunting – listening and watching for the signs in yourself and in others that love is entering your life. You must turn over every rock, watch for every clue that may lead you to your heart's desire. The world is beckoning you onwards to fulfil your dreams; remain alert so you can heed its call. Be persistent and joyful as you search; everything comes to those who wait. Soon, love will appear, quietly and completely enveloping your life.

Now you can begin to touch, smell and taste love

around you; it fills your senses. This is the time to respond to it with all your heart, openly without cynicism, without idealizing it, remembering that it is transitory and will change.

What you do in the Season of Hope is the first step towards realizing the dreams that you experienced in the time before. You must keep in mind where you want to be and celebrate the first uncertain steps without getting waylaid on your journey by the heady feelings that love brings you. You are sowing the seeds of your hopes.

The love charms in this section will help you learn how to listen to the rhythms and unspoken resonances of your relationship, whatever stage it is in.

ABOVE: *The Season of Hope is a good time of the year to look deeply into your partner's eyes and listen to his or her heart.*

RIGHT: *Spring is the season of beginnings and new growth.*

Love, when it is fresh, fills and feeds your soul and allows you to be innocent for a while, enraptured by the pulse of your heart. You hope, against hope, that this is the answer to your dreams and that it will take you to where you want to be. It is the nature of love to hope, and this is the season to believe and to act to fulfil that hope.

A Time for Listening

Spend some time thinking about all the things that you would like to share with the person you love, things you have dreamed of that you would like to happen. Make some notes if you need to, but not as if it was a list of demands or an agenda for a meeting, use keywords to describe your feelings. Suggest to your lover that they do the same.

When you have focussed on your own wishes and feelings, think about what the person in your life has said during the last few days. What has he told you about himself, what has been discussed? Did you listen to his needs? Did you truly understand the meaning? Think about his wishes and desires in the same way that you thought about your own. Make notes if you find it helpful. Remember that in this season people often become caught up in the whirl of love, and misunderstand each other, or they may become disconnected from reality and exist in a dream world.

Once you have meditated on yourself and your lover, you could think about sharing your notes with your loved one. You

BELOW: *Use the Season of Hope to make some time to talk, without the tv, radio or phones to distract and interrupt you.*

might find that you have recalled his concerns really accurately, you might not! Use what you have learned to help make the effort to move away from dreaming into the world that exists about you, from winter to spring, even if it is sometimes harsh. This is a season of listening and sharing.

During this time you are laying the seeds for the future. You are setting the boundaries, the expectations of a burgeoning relationship. If you do not hear what the other person dreams of, if you do not hear his thoughts, then you will never know whether the path that you walk will take you closer to or further away from that person. Only by listening to what the other person's ideas and needs are, are you able truly to give your heart to him. Later in the relationship you will be able to listen more easily, but now you need to be careful and patient.

Love Ritual

FIND A SPACE OUTDOORS WHERE YOU FEEL AT PEACE WITH YOURSELF. LOOK AT ANY TREES AROUND YOU. NOTICE HOW UNIQUE EACH ONE IS. SEE IF A TREE CATCHES YOUR ATTENTION AND GATHER A FALLEN BRANCH OR TWIG FROM IT. USE THE BRANCH AS A TALISMAN TO REMIND YOU OF THE TREE AND THAT SPECIAL PLACE.

A LISTENING MEDITATION

This is a meditation for listening and looking, reminding you that there is always more to see. You will never see all there is to see on a beach, in a tree or in a person. You must always be looking harder because there is something extraordinary hidden in every tiny item. Do this meditation in the early morning, if possible.

1 Kneel, sitting on your heels, with your toes behind you and your back and neck straight. Light a candle or some incense to focus your concentration. Rest your hands on your thighs or knees. This should feel relatively comfortable. Close your eyes and breathe slowly. Relax and try to empty your mind. Start by listening to the noises around you. Try to pick out each distinguishing sound. Listen harder. What background sounds can you notice? Perhaps there are some which you were not even aware of before.

2 Now take three slow breaths and empty your mind again. Open your eyes and look at the smoke or the flame. Do not move your head, just see whatever it is in front of your eyes. Look closer and notice the textures, movement, shadows and patterns. Take three slow breaths and empty your mind before moving. You can repeat this mental exercise while eating, noticing all the tastes in each mouthful of food, or while dressing, noticing all the textures as they brush against your skin.

Maypoles

THE MAYPOLE IS AN ANCIENT SYMBOL OF FERTILITY AND THE JOINING OF THE MALE AND FEMALE TOGETHER. THE ORIGINS OF THE MAYPOLE HARK BACK TO ANCIENT TIMES WHEN TREE SPIRITS WERE WORSHIPPED. THE FIRST MAYPOLES WERE TALL SLENDER TREES, USUALLY BIRCH, WHICH HAD THEIR BRANCHES CUT OFF.

The custom of dancing around the maypole is an ancient fertility rite, which is still performed today on village greens and at spring fetes. The oldest written references to maypoles come in the 14th century, but since these make it clear they are referring to a generations-old custom it is assumed that the maypole dates back to the days of the Angles and Saxons, who came to Britain from Germany and began to settle around 550AD. This theory is given some strength by the fact that similar customs continue in areas of Germany to this day.

The maypole itself is seen as a phallic symbol representing the planting of the god's phallus into the mother earth's womb, thereby illustrating the bringing forth of new life.

Dancing around the maypole was once a very merry and frivolous affair, yet today's maypole dancing with its colourful ribbons is a relatively modern dance, only dating back to the 19th century. However, this new adaptation is now accepted as a very important aspect of the maypole dance. By taking two ribbons each and weaving them together in an intricate and well-rehearsed pattern, the dancers weave the strands together to form a new combined element, perhaps to represent the partnership between men and women. Use the symbolism of the maypole in the love charm opposite, selecting a tree that has particular meaning for your wishes or desires.

LEFT: *The Maying festival has been enjoyed for centuries.* Come Join in the Maypole Dance *by Henry John Yeend King (1855–1924).*

Trees for Love

APPLE TREES HAVE BEEN ASSOCIATED WITH LOVE AND MARRIAGE SINCE CLASSICAL GREECE. THE CELTS ALSO LINKED THE APPLE TREE WITH LOVE, HEATHER WITH ROMANCE, ALDER WITH PASSION AND BIRCH WITH RENEWAL AND FERTILITY. HOLLY IS SEEN AS BRINGING GOOD LUCK, HAZEL IS ASSOCIATED WITH WISDOM, AND ROWAN WITH PROTECTION.

A Maypole Love Charm

This love charm is a symbol of the beginning and hope of spring. Make this small version as a love token to signify the hope that the lives of you and your loved one will be interlinked in the coming cycle. This charm demonstrates your intention to work together with the other person, to weave your paths together, so that both your dreams are fulfilled.

1 Take the lengths of ribbon and secure them around the top of the stick using the thread or wool. Hold the stick firmly in place and lay out the ribbons in the four directions.

2 Wind the north and south ribbons clockwise and the east and west ribbons anti-clockwise around the wood. Weave two sets of adjacent ribbons together as shown; north ribbon over west and south over east.

3 Repeat weaving the ribbons around the stick, crossing alternate, adjacent pairs in a continuous pattern until you reach the base.

4 Secure the ends with thread or wool. Leave the ribbon ends free, or tie beads or stones into them to make the charm a unique and special gift.

41

WISHING STONE LOVE CHARM

IN THE SEASON OF HOPE YOU STRIKE OUT TOWARDS YOUR DREAMS, WISHING THEY WOULD COME TRUE. A WISHING STONE IS AN OBJECT THAT CAN CONTAIN ALL OF YOUR WISHES AND THOSE OF THE PERSON YOU LOVE, HOLDING THEM TOGETHER IN ONE SYMBOLIC PLACE.

As a love charm, a wishing stone reminds you of the wishes you share with another and gives a physical way to remember them. By using a wishing stone as a talisman to hold your wishes, you are taking the first step towards bringing them into reality. When you present the love charm, tell the person you love about the wishes it holds and invite him or her to fill it with their wishes, too. Listen to your partner's wishes, and ask them to listen to yours. Perhaps each of you can fill the stone with new wishes as they come to you. Whenever you see the stone, remember each one of the wishes it contains, and think about how you might make one of them come to pass.

BELOW: *The wishing stone is an ancient charm for making your dreams come true. Often a person would make a wish as he dropped the stone into the sea or a wishing well.*

1 Think of three wishes you have, wishes you would like to share with a special person. Imagine simple patterns or shapes that remind you of those wishes.

2 Paint the patterns on the stone, using colours you feel the person you love would appreciate. Paint all over its surface using all the colours, then leave it to dry. Place your stone where you can see it and remember what it holds.

SEASON OF HOPE VALENTINE

St Valentine's day falls in the Season of Hope, on 14 February. Harness all the energy of this day and make your own valentine, whether it is to keep as a symbol of the love you have to give, or a gift for the person you love.

Mid February has been dedicated to love since the Romans celebrated Lupercalia, a fertility festival. In 496AD the pope declared 14 February to be St Valentine's day but it wasn't until the 15th century that the day was associated with romantic love. A storebought Valentine card is a good way to tell someone how you feel, but making your own, and transferring your hopes and dreams as you do so, is a much more potent love token.

You will need

BROWN AND SILVER GIFT WRAP

PALE PINK CARD

SPRAY ADHESIVE

BRIGHT PINK, LIGHT PINK AND SILVER PAPER

GLUE STICK

SCISSORS (SCALLOP-EDGED IF YOU HAVE THEM)

1 Stick brown and silver gift wrap to pale pink card. Cut a 20 x 13cm/8 x 5½in rectangle from the card with a craft knife and ruler. Score and fold the card in the middle.

2 Cut two shapes as shown above, one from bright pink paper and one from light pink paper. Cut two slits in each as shown. Weave the straight ends of the heart sections together. As you do this, think of the person you love and what you feel about them.

3 Cut a 4.5cm/1¾in square of silver paper. Next cut a 5.5cm/2¼in square of bright pink paper using scallop-edged scissors if you have them. Stick the silver square on the bright pink square. Stick the bright pink square to the card front. Stick the heart to the silver square with an adhesive foam pad. When your card is finished, hold it to your heart and transfer your wishes to it.

Season of Passion

When you can see and hear the other person for who he or she is, when you are completely open with him or her and it is reciprocal, then you are in a safe place to express the passion that fills your heart. This is the season of heat, of dance, of rapture and cries of joy. This is the season where you can leap into your dreams wholeheartedly, where you can reap the benefits of sharing and listening. Now you know the other person and know that your hearts beat to the same rhythm.

This is the season when two people move as one, when your passion for life spills over. Passion and love can be forces of tremendous change and it often takes courage to ride this season to its peak. Never be afraid to express your feelings, or embrace the other person's feelings with joy. When there are moments of disharmony, remember the hopes you shared before, and remember how to listen and not to judge. At this time, if it is appropriate, you may decide to follow the heat of passion in lovemaking. This is a period when you give with every part of your being, without regrets, guilt or disrespect.

In this time of rising passion, you lay your soul bare to the other person. You find the courage to show your vulnerability because this is the only way to share your deepest self with him or her. Sometimes when you feel vulnerable, you can put up defences, as the ego reluctantly relinquishes control of the heart, and your past wounds, if still healing, are revealed. With these defences there is often irrational anger, a closing down and withdrawal of the person. You must always respect someone when you walk close to painful places. Let him or her be angry and offer understanding. Love understands grief, as it is part of the natural cycle.

In this season you must be mindful of the joy and the pain in the places where you light the fires of passion.

ABOVE: *In the Season of Passion, when nature flowers in summer, you become gloriously alive, your love can grow and you express your love with every fibre of your being.*

RIGHT: *Now is the time to open your heart and release your passion, without fear of the consequences, just as the crops in the fields reach their full growing potential.*

> It isn't possible to love and part. You will wish that it was. You can transmute love, ignore it, muddle it, but you can never pull it out of you. I know by experience that the poets are right: love is eternal.
> E.M. Forster, "A Room with a View"

44

A Time for Expression

With passion comes expression. Let your body, the truest expression of your soul, demonstrate your feelings.
Try to become used to expressing yourself openly, in words and deeds. Be confident in your
feelings, no one else may judge them, they are not right or wrong.

Dance to some music you enjoy and feel comfortable moving your body. Experiment with moving different parts of it. Start by dancing with the head and neck, then with the shoulders. Bring in your arms, elbows, wrists and fingertips so that your whole upper body is in motion. Then introduce the movement of the spine, the sway of your hips, the thousand ways to move your legs and feet, even your toes. If you cannot move some parts of your body, move as much as you are able to. Do not be self-conscious. Just let your whole body express your feelings with the music; hold some fabric so that it follows your movements. Dance for no one but yourself, becoming comfortable with every pore of your body speaking your heart. When you are with others be conscious of their physical presence; can you sense what they need? Would they

benefit from a hug or a touch of hands? If you find it difficult to sense intuitively what might be appropriate, then do not be afraid to ask. Touch is one of the most important gifts we have to offer, by touching someone we remind them that they belong; that they are wanted and loved in this world. Be aware of your own needs, too. Speak up when you want a hug or even a massage. By asking for physical attention, you open the door for others to open up their hearts and express their love in a physical way.

Spend some time remembering the feeling of the person you love, retrace his or her skin in your mind. If you want to, spend some time together exploring how each of you feels. Sit close together, facing each other, both of you with your eyes closed. Run your fingers over each other, tracing the outline and contours of your faces. Then, when you are apart, see if you can recall these contours.

BELOW: *Cuddling your partner helps to bond a relationship.*
BELOW RIGHT: *Dancing encourages freedom of expression.*

MEDITATION FOR RELAXATION

This meditation is to aid relaxation and is designed to remind you of the sensation of your own body. Everyone is unique and you should take pleasure from this difference and offer it with joy. Play some relaxing music while performing this mediation to feel the full benefit.

I Lie down on the floor, with something soft, such as a blanket or rug, beneath your back. Place your hands beneath your lower back, then raise the upper body onto your elbows, stretch your neck back and your feet forward and feel all your muscles tighten. Then lie back on the floor, relaxed, with your hands by your sides. Close your eyes.

2 Start with your toes. Breathing in, clench them up as hard as you can and then as you breathe out, release them. Next, do the same with your ankles. As you breathe in, tense to bring your feet off the floor, then relax as you breathe out.

3 Work your way slowly up your body, clenching and relaxing your knees, your thighs, your bottom, your stomach, your fingers and your shoulders, all the way up to your head. Finally, try to clench the scalp of your head and then relax it. Take a long, slow breath and relax. Notice your body again. If there are parts which still feel a little tense, repeat the exercise with them.

4 As you practice you will be able to relax parts of your body more easily. This exercise also heightens an awareness of your own body, helping you to feel it more intimately.

Lavender Love Charm

FLOWERS AND GARLANDS HAVE BEEN USED BY MANY CULTURES TO SIGNIFY THE ETERNAL BOND BETWEEN TWO PEOPLE, A CIRCLE THAT UNITES THEM. LAVENDER SIGNIFIES LOVE AND DEVOTION, AND WHEN PRESENTED AS A GIFT ALSO OFFERS THE PROMISE OF NEW ADVENTURE.

It was customary for lovers to hang a garland on the door of their beloved on the first day of summer. Couples used to wear crowns of flowers on their marriage day, and it is still traditional for a bride today to wear some kind of floral headress. This heart-shaped lavender wreath can hang on a door, inside or out, to signify the Season of Passion, its scent evoking high summer days that last for ever, lavender bushes shimmering against the blue sky, the bees blundering in and out among the flowers, stirring up the intense, sweet aromas. When you give your love charm, tell the person you love how you feel about the bond that you share.

You will need

TO MAKE A HEART MEASURING ABOUT
30 x 30CM/12 x 12IN
120 LARGE LAVENDER HEADS
SECATEURS OR SCISSORS
FLORISTS' REEL WIRE OR ANY
FINE WIRE
GARDEN WIRE
FLORISTS' TAPE
GREEN STRING (YARN)

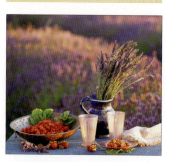

LEFT: *A warmly-scented lavender field in high summer would be the perfect place for a romantic evening, watching the sun set.*

I Cut the stems to about 2.5cm/1in and make bunches of about six heads each, securing them with florists' wire.

2 Make a hook at each end of a piece of garden wire about 60cm/2 ft long. Link to make a circle, make a dip at the top edge and bend the wire into a heart shape.

3 Using florists' tape, bind a bunch of lavender to the bottom of the wire heart. Bind the next bunch a little further up the wire. Continue until you reach the centre top, then start again at the bottom and work up.

4 Tie a bunch of lavender with green raffia and tie on to the bottom of the wreath. Pass the raffia to the back to catch the stems and then secure at the front with a bow.

Eternity Band Love Charm

As a symbol of the bond that you share with a person, you can present him or her with an eternity band. It is made as a single circle and then cut in half; each person then wears one half of the band, signifying how the two people are one in their hearts. This is a very potent sign and you should think carefully whether it is the right time for you to share this with someone.

When you present this charm to someone you love, you may want to do so with some ceremony, for example during a meal, in the atmosphere of a lighted candle or in a special place. Tell your lover your feelings and your passions as you present the charm and explain what this eternity band signifies to you. If he accepts the gift, cut the band in half between knots using scissors. Each of you can then tie the other person's band into place and, if it feels right, seal the final knot with a kiss.

1 Begin by spending some time quietly, preparing your thoughts and capturing the intent with which you wish to fill the eternity band. Gather up small beads and shells and any other charms that you feel should be a part of the band.

2 Cut the length of thong or lace so that you can wrap it roughly three times around your wrist. Leave about 2cm (¾in) and tie a knot at one end of the thong. Think about the pattern that you want to make.

3 Begin threading on the beads and charms. Group the beads together by tying a knot in the thong or lace, then thread on the beads. Tie another knot to secure them into the pattern. Do this at frequent intervals.

4 When you have only 2.5–5cm (1–2in) left, tie the last knot to secure the charms, then tie the two ends together.

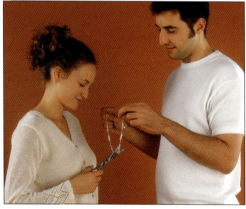

5 Present the charm to your partner, cut the wristband in half and tie one half around one another's wrists.

Season of Fulfilment

Once passion has risen, peaked and found its natural balance, you will find there is a huge and wonderful space created between the person you love and yourself. It is a space where you are nurtured and where possibilities exist you had not even dreamed of before.

This is a time when you can reflect on your journey. You have the time to learn from all those mistakes in the past seasons. You may realize that you have reached a place which was not part of your dream and in which you must now find peace.

The Season of Fulfilment is associated with autumn. In the time after passion you become fulfilled and find calmness in your life. It is here that the true healing of love occurs. This can be a painful process as love discovers the deeper aspects of your heart and the healing of old wounds occurs.

Now you must also accept that this contentment is transitory. It will not last and should not last. If you are content for too long, you forget

your dreams and stop the cycle of love from carrying on. If you get stuck here, if the cycle stops, so too will love and you may wake up one day and find it has left you completely.

In the time of fulfilment you are rejoicing in the journey so far, but also preparing for new dreams and letting go of old ones which you find you no longer yearn for. Autumn is a time of acceptance and honesty, and the knowledge that all things change and some things must perish for others to live.

LEFT: *The Season of Fulfilment is a time for taking stock and reviewing the events of the past year.*

RIGHT: *In autumn, the natural world withers and dies to make way for new growth.*

Nothing else matters much – not wealth, nor learning, nor even health – without this gift: the spiritual capacity to keep zest in living. This is the creed of creeds, the final deposit and distillation of all important faiths: that you should be able to believe in life.

Harry Emerson Fosdick

A Time for Self Reflection

This is the season for looking at yourself carefully in the mirror, noticing the changes that have happened and accepting who you are and where you are. Remember the insights you achieved in the previous season, and assess them in the light of this new Season of Fulfilment. Think about and value the self knowledge that you will inevitably acquire during the cycle.

Spend time alone thinking about what your dreams and hopes were at the beginning of the cycle, the time when you were last dreaming about who you are and what you want to do and be. Think about whether you have fulfilled those dreams or whether they still have meaning for you.

Write down those dreams that no longer represent what you desire. Now think about yourself and how you have changed. Are there things that you don't like about yourself? What things are you glad to have gained from love? Write down all the things that you feel you have lost. As you write

down each one, try to remember one thing you have gained that replaces it. By opening your heart to another, you have looked deeper into yourself. Finally, take a look at your habits. Are you fixed in your ways? Are there habits that prevent you from accepting aspects of your relationship? Write them down and make an effort to let go of them, thinking of a possibility that may occur by doing things differently.

Take all those words and put them to rest. Either build a fire for them, or bury them. As you do so, remember all the wonderful gifts that the relationship has brought you.

BELOW: *Take a few days to think about your hopes and dreams; make notes as you do so. Reflect on what your assessment is.*

BELOW: *When you have collected your thoughts, let go of them by burning or burying them, thinking as you do about the positive elements.*

MEDITATION FOR CHANGE

As you reach a time of change, you often find you become tense and full of dark thoughts as you resist the
need to change. You may become angry, not wanting to let the cycle move on, preferring to keep the status quo.
This is a meditation for releasing any dark clouds of frustration and replacing them with warmth and light, so that you are
ready to accept whatever is ahead. It is especially good if practised first thing in the morning.

1 Stand with your feet shoulder-width apart and parallel. Keep your back straight, head up, and your arms relaxed in front of you. Bend your knees slightly and close your eyes. Feel heavy in your body, sink your weight downwards so that you are firmly connected with the ground.

2 Bring your arms up in a wide circle and breathe in slowly and deeply through your nose. As you do so, imagine that the air you breathe in is full of white light, happiness and all the bright possibilities that the day holds before you.

3 Bring your hands together in front of you in the prayer position, then turn your palms downwards and bring your arms down in front of you, breathing out through your mouth. As you do so, imagine the air you are expelling is grey and dark, full of all the worries and frustrations of the past day or moments before. Let your hands come to rest at your sides again and repeat the exercise twice more.

Protection Charm

IN MANY CULTURES GIVING A CLOAK, BLANKET OR SCARF SIGNIFIES THE OFFER OF PROTECTION, THAT THE PERSON WHO GIVES WILL BE RESPONSIBLE FOR THE WELLBEING OF THE OTHER.

You can give a decorated piece of fabric that symbolizes a cloak as a love charm to signify that you will always respect the other person. You are there should he need you, but equally you will remain folded away if he needs to be alone.

The size of the fabric can be large enough for physical warmth – perhaps you could make a quilt with your own symbols – or it can be as small as a token handkerchief or scarf. A cloak has a deep connection with the blankets or quilts that you were wrapped in as a baby, and offer protection and peace to the heart.

BELOW: Making a quilt, using scraps of fabric from your lives, and sewn with appropriate symbols and shapes, can be a real act of love.

Think about the pattern or decorations to use on the fabric. For example, do you want an emblem signifying your love in the centre of the piece, or do you want to decorate only the borders? You could choose an animal or plant motif that you feel is associated with the person, or has attributes that you wish to include in your protection.

When you have finished give it to the person you love as a folded parcel. Ask him to accept it as a token of your intentions. Explain what your thoughts were while making it and what they are now. Tell them that they can remind themselves through touching the fabric token that you are always there when you are needed.

PROTECTIVE MOTIFS

FLOWERS AND ANIMALS
THAT SYMBOLIZE LOVE:
ALOE: PROTECTION
EDELWEISS: DEVOTION
HELIOTROPE: ETERNAL,
NEVER-ENDING LOVE
HOLLY: HOPE AND JOY
MYRTLE: MARRIAGE
AND TRUE LOVE
ROSE: DESIRE, LOVE
YARROW: EVERLASTING
LOVE
HORSE: FREEDOM, TRAVEL
TIGER: PASSION, POWER
AND DEVOTION
WOLF: LOYALTY
MOTH: FAITHFULNESS

SYMBOLIC CLOAK

THIS SMALL PIECE OF FABRIC CAN HOLD WHATEVER PROTECTIVE SYMBOLISM YOU WISH TO
GIVE IT, WHETHER YOU CREATE AN ABSTRACT DESIGN OR USE A MOTIF.

YOU WILL NEED

SQUARE OF FABRIC
SOFT PENCIL
NEEDLE AND THREAD
SMALL PIECES OF FABRIC,
BEADS AND CHARMS
PAINTBRUSH
FABRIC PAINTS OR
EMBROIDERY THREAD
(FLOSS)

RIGHT: *Giving a protective love charm symbolizes the intention to respect your partner through life.*

1 Select the material and colour carefully, imagining what will feel the most warming to the recipient.

2 Draw out the pattern on the cloth, using a pencil. Think about the images and symbols.

3 Sew on the pieces of fabric you have chosen. Tie on beads and other charms if you feel they are needed.

4 Now use either fabric paints or embroidery thread (floss) to fill in the pattern.

57

Talking Stick Charm

The talking stick is a Native American tool to help people communicate during difficult times. Traditionally it was a carved wooden stick but it can be made of any material. Here a paper scroll is used as a communication charm.

A talking stick love charm can be made for any unspoken problem. Use it as a way of moving forward in a relationship, accepting changes as they are encountered. To use a talking stick, place it in front of both of you. If one of you wishes to speak, you can then pick up the stick. The other person must listen intently and respectfully in silence. When the speaker

BELOW: The process of creating a talking stick may be enough to break the communication barrier you have been suffering from. When you have finished using it, burn it to symbolize moving on.

has finished he or she replaces the stick on the ground for the other person to pick up and speak, if they wish to do so. Here, for this Season of Fulfilment and healing, the stick is made as a scroll of paper.

Consider what inscription you would like to put on the scroll. This will be hidden during the time you are talking. After you have both said what it is that you need to share, the scroll can be read by the other person, or burnt to symbolize that the issue is forgotten or resolved.

Create two talking scrolls, if you wish, one for each person. Write your concerns down, then exchange the scrolls and read each other's, before you start sharing what you want to say.

"When we can talk about our feelings, they become less overwhelming, less upsetting, and less scary. The people we trust with that important talk can help us know that we are not alone."
Fred Rogers

1 Using the coloured pencils or paints, draw out the inscription on the paper. Spend time designing and choosing the words or symbols, remembering that they indicate talking and listening to the person you love.

2 Paint on the design and let it dry. As you paint each brushstroke, think about listening to the person you love, and about letting go of a problem so that you can both live without its shadow over you.

3 Roll up the paper into a scroll, and secure it with some wool (yarn) or ribbon. The symbols, along with your intentions, are now bound within the roll of the charm.

4 Present the charm to the person you love and suggest how it may be used. If you both feel the need to talk about something that is difficult, use it as described, so that one listens while the other speaks, holding the stick. When you both feel you have finished, throw the talking stick on to a fire. Watch the flames devour it, symbolizing the healing and end to the issue.

You will need

COLOURED PAINTS, FELT TIPS, OR
PENCILS
PAINTBRUSH
PIECE OF PAPER OR THIN CARDBOARD
COLOURED RIBBON, LEATHER CORD
OR WOOL (YARN)

FINAL WORD

LOVE IS A GIFT THAT WE ALL SHARE, AS FRIENDS, AS FAMILY, AS ALL CREATURES LIVING TOGETHER ON THIS WONDERFUL EARTH. AT EVERY MOMENT WE ARE GIVEN A CHANCE TO EXPRESS THAT CONNECTION, WHETHER IT BE HUGGING A FRIEND OR OFFERING WHAT WE HAVE TO THOSE WHO GO WITHOUT.

To love someone is a truly precious and joyous feeling, but it is also one that will constantly challenge you to listen to and learn from. Love is a living thing. When you stop listening and give up learning then the beauty of it withers and fades.

Love charms are gifts, tools and special places where you can remind yourself of the beauty that you share with someone, or reawaken something that has shrivelled up from neglect. They can help turn your dreams into a reality and take you on in the cycle to create more dreams and more special moments in your life.

It sometimes takes courage and determination to follow the cycle of love. You must always be listening to the voice of your heart so that you can move ever forwards towards your dream. There may be times when you must weep for what you have lost, but there will be other times when you will cry out with joy at what you have gained. Everyone walks the cycle of love, and its changing seasons carry them onwards to happiness and the life of their dreams.

Love charming is an art that everyone possesses; they are born with its knowledge beating inside them. You can practise this art of bringing love to everyone around you as part of the everyday world. In so doing, you become the warm, loving person that you truly are at heart.

May you walk a path of beauty and love
every moment of your life
and so live the life of your dreams.

LEFT: *The lovers, Paolo and Francesca da Rimini, 1867 by Dante Gabriel Rossetti (1828–1882).*

RIGHT: *Venus Verticordia, 1864–68 by Dante Gabriel Rossetti.*

Table of Rune Meanings

Rune	Letter	Name	Table of Rune Symbols
F	F	Feoh	Wealth, riches and blessings for a new beginning
ᚢ	U	Ur	The strength and perseverance of the wild ox
ᚦ	Th	Thorn	Protection of thorns around the heart
ᚨ	A	Ansuz	Speaking and telling of charms and dreams
ᚱ	R	Rad	Turning the wheel and cycle of love
ᚲ	K	Ken	Bringing the light of understanding and acceptance
ᚷ	G	Gyfu	The giving and sharing of equals
ᚹ	W	Wyn	Joy of life when you are walking the path to your dreams
ᚺ	H	Hagal	Destruction of the old and letting go of the past
ᚾ	N	Nyd	The need for love, which burns in your heart
ᛁ	I	Is	Sudden endings, frozen and broken in a moment
ᛃ	J	Jera	Celebrating the seasons of love
ᛇ	Z	Eihwaz	Eternity of love and its cycle of creation, death and renewal
ᛈ	P	Peorth	The freedom of choice to make your own choices
ᛉ	X	Elhaz	Protection and resistance against ill-intended actions
ᛊ	S	Sigel	The sun at dawn, bringing light to the dark places in your life
ᛏ	T	Tiwaz	Justice and truth everywhere beneath the spinning sky
ᛒ	B	Beorc	The birth of fertile new beginnings
ᛖ	E	Ehwaz	The loyalty and faithfulness of the horse
ᛗ	M	Man	Connection of each person as human beings on Earth
ᛚ	L	Lagu	Water to help your life and love grow
◇	Ng	Ing	Spreading the boundless light of your heart out into the world
ᚨ	O	Odal	Creating a space in your life which you can call your own
ᛞ	D	Dag	Welcoming in bright intentions and warding off dark ones

Table of Tree Symbolism

Tree	Letter	Old Name	Symbolic Meanings
Birch	B	Beth	Sweep away the dark places in your heart to allow something new to grow
Rowan	L	Luis	The protection of fire against the dark
Ash	N	Nion	Force of creation allowing you to form reality from your dreams
Alder	F	Fearn	Emotional strength and perseverance
Willow	S	Saille	Flowing, cleansing water of healing
Hawthorn	H	Huath	Birth of possibilities and hope
Oak	D	Duir	Doorway through to understanding of the heart
Holly	T	Tinne	Never-ending watchfulness
Hazel	C	Coll	Listening to your dreams and taking the initiative to make them happen
Bramble	M	Muin	Bringing about change in your life and dreams
Ivy	G	Gort	Determination and strength in walking around the cycle of love
Reed	Ng	Ngetal	Speaking and writing words from your heart
Elder	R	Ruis	Calling the magic of love into your life
Apple	Q	Quert	Sharing the limitless love in the world
Blackthorn	St	Straif	Projection of your heart and feelings out into the world
Elm	A	Ailm	Growing onwards and upwards to rise above the difficulties in life
Gorse	O	Onn	Hope of what love will bring
Heather	U	Ur	Renewing and refreshing old or tired love
Poplar	E	Eadha	Directing your feelings towards a particular person or place in your life
Yew	I	Iubhar	Learning from the past and letting it go

INDEX